My Body Wants to Be Healthy

By Nancy Shriver
Illustrated by Emelia Sabine Schmidt

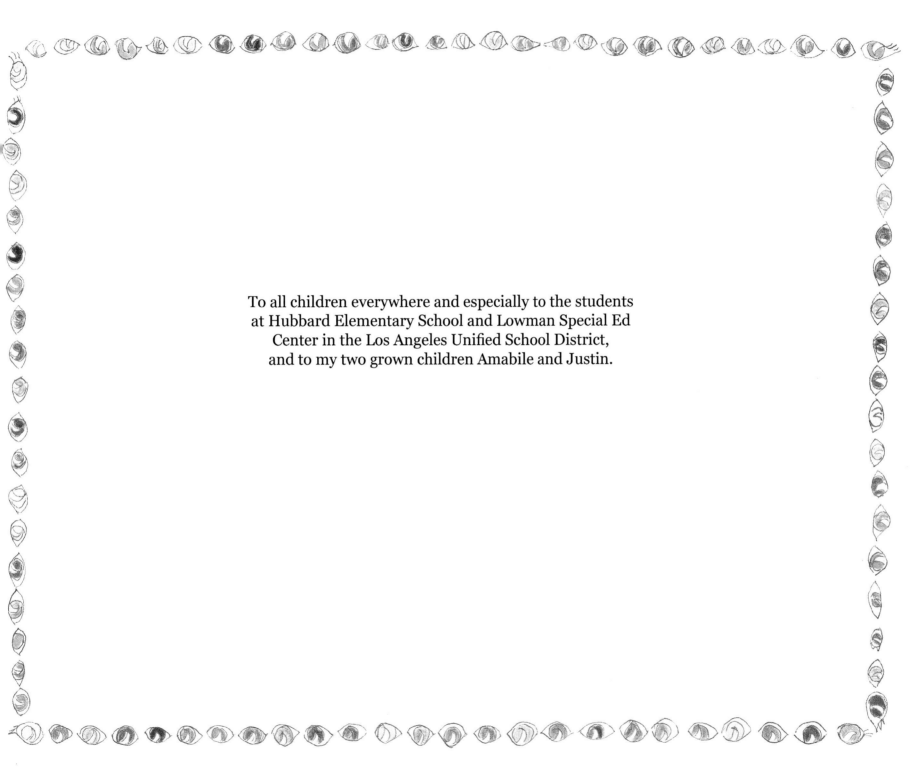

To all children everywhere and especially to the students
at Hubbard Elementary School and Lowman Special Ed
Center in the Los Angeles Unified School District,
and to my two grown children Amabile and Justin.

My body wants to be healthy!

My body is amazing. It does many things like seeing, hearing, breathing, eating...

...and so much more.

The smartest people in the world are not totally sure how it works,
but they know that my body wants to be healthy.

If I fall and scrape my knee - ouch - it hurts. That hurt tells my body that my knee needs healing. So I clean my knee and my body takes over. Everyday the scrape gets better and smaller until, *Presto!* it is not there at all.

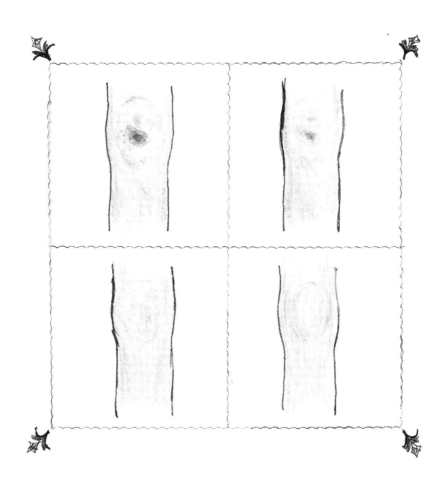

That is because *my body wants to be healthy.*

My body lets me know when it needs something.

Sometimes, my stomach feels empty. I need to eat. And when I feel full, I stop eating. Sometimes, I yawn. My body may be telling me that I need fresh air, or I might need to breathe slower and deeper, or maybe, I just need more sleep.

If I feel a pain in my muscles, it might mean I need to stretch and exercise.

If I listen and pay attention, I can learn to sense what my body needs.

My body wants to be healthy.

My body likes to laugh and play, and move, move, move.

When I find something I love to do, it is easier to keep on doing it.

I love walking, skipping, dancing, swimming, climbing or other great activities.

Some of my friends like playing basketball or tennis. Some like ice skating, climbing trees, or riding a bike. There are so many fun games to play and practice.

I like to
move, move, move
and my body likes it too.

My body wants to be healthy.

And food, yum, yum!

Fresh food and water help my body to grow and help my brain to learn. My body loves vegetables. I can make salads with lettuce, cucumbers, avocados, and green peas. I can add tomatoes, carrots, and raisins or even some pumpkin seeds.

fresh and ripe

I can eat fruit almost any time, like blueberries, strawberries, grapes, or a banana. And I can pick an apple, a peach, a plum or a pear, fresh and ripe from a tree.

Friends and family are part of the fun.
Doing things together helps us stay happy and healthy.

We can play games together, talk and laugh together and even play with pets.
We can have family dinners together and invite our friends for tea.

When we do things together it brings love, happiness and health.

All of our bodies want to be healthy.

I like to run and play and laugh. I like to eat good food and have fun with people I love. I listen to my body and it tells me what it needs.

I am healthy.

My body is healthy!

My body really wants to be healthy and happy. Teenagers and grown-ups learn that in science classes. They learn about something called "homeostasis".

That is a big word that means the body wants to work well. It means if something happens, the body naturally wants to return to normal health.

"Hom-e-o-sta-sis."

A great word. Maybe we can remember it and surprise a science teacher one day.

Nancy Shriver is a school nurse and has worked with all ages of children within the Los Angeles Unified School District in California. She also is a Yoga instructor and has long been interested in how food, exercise and attitude can contribute to healthy living.

Emelia Sabine Schmidt has led an exciting life so far. Possibly her first work of art was a fantastic toy makeover in which she painted a bouncy horse blue. Emelia lives in Viroqua, a small town in rural Wisconsin with a population of 4,500. She lives with her mom, pop, brother, 2 dogs, 3 hamsters and assorted mice who live in the walls. Emelia participates in setting the table, letting the dogs out, and improving the tree house. She is reading all the good books and figuring out what her purpose in life may be.

"The natural healing force in each one of us is the greatest force in getting well."

-Hippocrates